Test Your Listening

Test Your

PENGUIN ENGLISH

Pearson Education Limited
Edinburgh Gate
Harlow
Essex CM20 2JE, England
and Associated Companies throughout the world.

ISBN 0 582 46908 2

First published 2002
Text copyright © Tricia Aspinall 2002

Designed and typeset by Pantek Arts Ltd, Maidstone, Kent
Test Your format devised by Peter Watcyn-Jones
Illustrations by Phil Healey, Gillian Martin, Peter Standley and Ross Thomson
Printed in Italy by Rotolito Lombarda

Acknowledgements
The author would like to thank Jake Allsop for his helpful advice and for being such a good listener.

Published by Pearson Education Limited in association with Penguin Books Ltd, both companies being subsidiaries of Pearson plc.

For a complete list of the titles available from Penguin English please visit our website at www.penguinenglish.com, or write to your local Pearson Education office or to: Marketing Department, Penguin Longman Publishing, 80 Strand, London WC2R 0RL.

Contents

To the student

If you want to improve your listening skills, you will find the tests in this book and the accompanying CD very useful. They will help you to practise listening to different voices and accents in a variety of situations.

The tests will also help you to listen in different ways. For example, you may need to listen to a conversation in order to decide who is speaking or what they think about a particular topic. On the other hand, you may need to listen out for a fact or detail in an announcement. At other times you must want to understand the general gist of what people are saying.

Many of the tests in this book include a tip about how to prepare for a task or what to listen out for. There are also notes and explanations about some of the words and phrases you will hear.

Some of the test tasks are probably similar to those you are used to doing in class. Others, such as picture stories and poems, have been included to add interest and variety. Whatever the task, the listening skills that are required are necessary, real world skills.

There are seven sections in this book. Each section covers a particular type of listening, from formal announcements to informal conversations and stories. Some recordings have two sets of tasks, and there are two recordings that have three sets. There is a key at the back of the book so that you can check your answers. Complete transcripts for all the listening tests are on pages 65 to 83. You can use these to check your answers or you may sometimes find it useful to read the transcript while you are listening to the recording.

You don't have to work through every test in the book in the order in which they appear. Choose topics that interest you but try to choose tests from each section of the book.

I hope you enjoy listening to these recordings and doing the tests. Don't forget to listen to English whenever you have the chance – English on the radio, on TV, on the street or anywhere. good luck with your listening!

Tricia Aspinall

1 Football round-up

Answer the questions by choosing football teams from the box.

Newcastle	Everton	Arsenal	Athletic Bilbao	Lazio
Middlesborough	Parma	West Ham		Blackburn Rovers
Ajax	Aston Villa	Leeds United	Chelsea	
Manchester United		Manchester City	Real Madrid	
	Liverpool	Ipswich Town		

1 Who beat Chelsea?

2 Which team scored the greatest number of goals?

3 Who won – Ajax or West Ham?

4 Who did Manchester United play?

5 Who lost to Ipswich town?

6 Which match was postponed?

7 Which two teams scored no goals?

8 Which team drew against Real Madrid?

Some common sporting terms:
fixture: a day fixed for a match
friendly: a match which is not part of a competition
draw: equal scores
postponed: put off to another date
soccer: football (i.e. not rugby)

2 Film talk

A   Listen to this radio presenter talking about films and match the words and phrases in list 1 to their meanings in list 2.

List 1

1	round-up
2	on general release
3	selected cinemas
4	adaptation
5	sequel

List 2

A	showing in some cinemas
B	different version
C	showing in most cinemas
D	follow-up
E	collection

B   Now complete sentences 1–5 using the words in list 1.

1   The film will be _____ from next week.

2   Here is a _____ of the latest films.

3   This film is a clever _____ of a popular stage play.

4   It is a disappointing _____ to the original film.

5   You may have some difficulty in getting to see this film as it is only showing at _____.

In the UK films are given a certificate. U means the film is unclassified and anyone can go. PG means 'parental guidance'. Anyone can go to these films but parents might not want to take young children. 12 is only for those over 12 years, 15 for those over 15 and 18 for those over 18.

3 Film talk (continued)

Listen again and fill in the gaps in the listings below using no more than three words each time.

FILM LISTINGS

Title	Certificate	Release Date	Cinema	Story
Gone (1) _in sixty_ _seconds_	15	(2) _____	General release	A retired (3) _____ is forced to do one more job.
Toy Story 2	U	16 May	(4) _____ _____	Woody is kidnapped by a (5) _____ _____
(6) _____ _____	(7) _____	16 May	(8) _____ cinemas	A story of (9) _____ and revenge.
Up at the Villa	(10) _____	(11) _____	Chichester cinema & selected cinemas	A triangular (12) _____ _____ .

Test tip: Read through the task carefully and try and predict what type of information you are listening for. For example: 2. Is a date or a day of the week required?

4 Have you seen these men?

Listen to this news report about two escaped prisoners and complete the details on this poster.

HAVE YOU SEEN THIS MAN?

(1) _____ Burke

Age: (2) _____   Height: (3) _____

This man is of (4) _____ build, has short

(5) _____ and (6) _____ eyes.

He has a (7) _____ of a (8) _____
on his left forearm.

Serving (9) _____ years for (10) _____
and manslaughter.

Some common words used to report crimes:

issue a warning: inform people about a possible danger

fatally injured: badly hurt, resulting in death

brutal murder: violent killing of someone

serving a sentence: undergoing a punishment given by a court of law

5 Have you seen these men? (continued)

Listen again and complete the details for the second man.

HAVE YOU SEEN THIS MAN?

(1) _____ Murray

Age: (2) _____ Height: (3) _____

This man is (4) _____ with a (5) _____
and a (6)_____ on his left cheek. He weighs 100 kg.

Serving (7) _____ years for (8) _____.

IF YOU SEE THESE MEN DO NOT (9) _____ THEM.

RING: (10) _____

6 Will the owner of ...

Listen to six public announcements and decide if you would hear them in an airport or a supermarket.

	AIRPORT	SUPERMARKET
Announcement 1		
Announcement 2		
Announcement 3		
Announcement 4		
Announcement 5		
Announcement 6		

7 Will the owner of ... (continued)

Listen again and match the objects to their pictures.

check-out – picture _____

check-in desk – picture _____

holdall – picture _____

blue cross – picture _____

security officer – picture _____

boarding card – picture _____

8 News headlines

Listen to these news headlines and answer the questions by choosing the best answer – a, b or c.

1 What happened to the lone yachtsman?

a) He ran into another boat.

b) He ran out of food.

c) He ran into a storm.

2 How did the motoring organisations respond to the rise in oil prices?

a) They were critical of the oil companies.

b) They were angry with the road hauliers.

c) They blamed the government.

3 How did the aid agencies respond to the crisis?

a) They appealed for supplies from the West.

b) They sent in fresh water and medicines.

c) They asked for the area to be declared a disaster zone.

4 What did the factory workers do after the accident?

a) They allowed the chickens to stay in the factory.

b) They helped to rescue the chickens from the water.

c) They exchanged the chickens for baskets they had made.

Test tip: Read the questions and each of the options <u>before</u> listening to the recording. Listen once and select your answer. Listen again and check you have chosen correctly.

9 News headlines (continued)

Choose the best heading for each of the four news items.

ANOTHER HIKE IN FUEL PRICES

INDIA ASKS FOR AID FOR FLOOD VICTIMS

KUHLEMEIER MAKES UNEXPECTED CALL ON IRELAND

MONSOON RAIN CAUSES FLOODS IN INDIA

CHICKEN RUN!

LONE YACHTSMAN PLUCKED FROM OCEAN

ROAD HAULIERS ANNOUNCE SUPPORT FOR OIL COMPANIES

FACTORY WORKERS STEAL CHICKEN CONSIGNMENT

Item 1 _____

Item 2 _____

Item 3 _____

Item 4 _____

Some useful words to help you listen to the news:

hike: increase

road haulier: lorry driver

at the pumps: at the petrol station

ruffle your feathers: disturb you

chicken-in-a-basket: a dish of chicken and chips served in a basket (used to be commonly served in British pubs)

10 News headlines (continued)

Listen again to the headlines and complete sentences 1–6 by choosing the most suitable word from the box to fill each gap.

1　During the voyage we _____ into stormy weather and had to find shelter.

2　It was thought best to _____ our efforts on finding somewhere safe to spend the night.

3　The lorry had _____ its load of animal feed on to the motorway.

4　We _____ from the ship at six in the morning and made our way to the hotel.

5　The introduction of new restrictions on TV advertising has _____ criticism from marketing companies.

6　After the hurricane hit the island it was over a week before electricity supplies were _____.

---

concentrate　　shed　　disembarked　　ran　　restored　　drawn

11 Stormy weather

Listen to this summary of a world weather forecast and decide whether the statements are true or false.

1	Tropical storm Hector is turning into a hurricane.	_T_
2	Hector is moving slowly towards Mexico.	_____
3	Hurricane Alberto is calming down.	_____
4	Alberto is approaching land at ninety miles per hour.	_____
5	Tropical storm Ewiniar is heading out to sea.	_____
6	Ewiniar is gaining in strength.	_____
7	Rain in Australia is expected to last all week.	_____
8	It will be mainly hot and dry in the Northern Alps.	_____
9	Scattered showers are expected in Great Britain.	_____
10	Florence is Europe's hottest spot.	_____

- Some useful weather vocabulary:
  scattered: far apart
  gusts: sudden brief increases in wind speed
  front: the edge of a mass of warm or cold air
  clear up: stop raining

- There are several words in this weather forecast which are typically American. In British English you are more likely to hear another word. Listen out for these words.

American English	British English
looks like	looks as if
located	situated
at present	at the moment
right now	at the moment
highs	highest temperatures

12 He's leaving home

Listen to the conversation between Tim and his mother and tick those things he says he will miss about his life at home.

1	his friends	☐
2	his mother's cooking	☐
3	his brother	☐
4	wearing clean, ironed clothes	☐
5	his old job	☐
6	walking the dog	☐
7	local shops	☐
8	borrowing the family car	☐
9	wearing a suit	☐
10	the laptop	☐

 Test tip: Read through the list of things Tim might miss and listen carefully. Remember they may be mentioned but not always because he will miss them!

13 Where does it hurt?

Listen to Mr Jenkins talking to his doctor and decide whether the statements are true or false.

1	He fell over his guitar.	_F_
2	The doctor examines both his feet.	_____
3	He can move his toes without pain.	_____
4	His ankle hurts a bit.	_____
5	His right foot is swollen.	_____
6	He needs to lose some weight.	_____
7	The receptionist will call the hospital.	_____
8	He can get some crutches from the hospital.	_____

- This man is visiting his **G.P. (General Practitioner)**. In the UK most people are registered with a local doctor. You need to see your G.P. before you go to a hospital or have any sort of treatment, except in an emergency.

- Some useful words when visiting the doctor:
  swollen: enlarged
  sprain: injury to a joint causing pain and swelling
  tender: painful when touched
  crutches: pair of poles used to support someone with injured legs or feet

14 All in a day's work

Match the pictures to the jobs.

1	Police officer	_____
2	Writer	_____
3	Farmer	_____
4	Waiter	_____
5	TV presenter	_____
6	Shopkeeper	_____
7	Journalist	_____
8	Vet	_____

15 All in a day's work (continued)

You will hear six people talking about their jobs. Decide who is speaking in each recording.

a	Vet	1	_c_
b	Farmer	2	____
c	Police officer	3	____
d	Shopkeeper	4	____
e	Waiter	5	____
f	Writer	6	____
g	TV presenter		
h	Journalist		

Test tip: First of all, read through the list of jobs and make sure you know what each job is about. Think about what these people might do in their daily work. Some jobs might have similar aspects such as a vet and a farmer.

16 All in a day's work (continued)

Listen again to the six recordings. Decide what each person is talking about.

a	working at night	1	_a_
b	working in a family business	2	____
c	working with holidaymakers	3	____
d	working with famous people	4	____
e	working alone	5	____
f	working with money	6	____
g	working for a bank		
h	working outside		

Some useful words about jobs:

unsocial hours: not standard working times, for instance working at night or weekends

late shift: period of work during the evening or night

take a break: stop working for a while

set up a business: start a business

bed and breakfast: a serivce offering a room to sleep in and breakfast next morning in a private house

17 Prepositional verbs

A You heard the verbs in list 1 in tests 15 and 16. Match them to the verbs in list 2 according to their meanings in the tests.

List 1	List 2
look after	fall over
settle in	remove
trip over	care for
take off	arrange
end up	finish up
set up	feel at home
set off	collect
pick up	leave

B Now complete these sentences with verbs from list 1. You may need to make changes to some verbs so that they fit the sentences.

1 Although she was quite old she _____ the dog very well.

2 Unfortunately he came last in the race because he _____ his shoe laces.

3 If you don't pass your exams you will _____ taking them again next year.

4 They _____ early to avoid the rush hour traffic.

5 He agreed to _____ the dry cleaning on his way home.

6 How long will it take to _____ the video recorder?

7 Are the children _____ to their new school?

8 I wish that woman in the front row would _____ her hat.

18 What if?

Listen to a man talking to a child about what she would do if she was a millionaire. Tick the things she says she will spend her money on.

 This sort of conversation with a child is often shown on UK television as part of a comedy programme so people can enjoy watching how 'cute' children can be. Do you have this sort of show in your country?

19 'Oh, really ...'

Listen to these short conversations and decide if speaker B sounds interested or bored. Put 'I' for interested and 'B' for bored.

1	A	I'm starting a new job on Monday.
	B	Are you? How exciting.

2	A	There's a new film on at the cinema. Do you want to go?
	B	Yes, I'd like that. Do we need to book?

3	A	The class is cancelled tonight. The teacher had an accident on the way here.
	B	Oh dear. Is she all right?

4	A	There's a party at Tom's tonight.
	B	Great. Am I invited?

5	A	I'm getting married in the summer.
	B	That's wonderful.

6	A	My results should be out tomorrow.
	B	Really? You must be worried.

7	A	There's a new student arriving today.
	B	Is there? I hope it's a girl.

8	A	I think there's a car coming up the drive.
	B	Right. I'll get my camera.

Test tip: Think about how you sound if you are interested. You will probably speak faster and your voice may go up and down more. When you are bored you will speak slower and your voice will not change very much.

20 Do sit down ...

You will hear a manager interviewing someone for a job. Listen out for these verbs, then use them to complete sentences 1–5.

| start off | stay in | work for | move on | look for |

1 Could you _____ by telling me a bit about yourself?

2 I didn't want to _____ that field.

3 I think it's time to _____.

4 I'm _____ more of a challenge.

5 You've been _____ a design company.

Useful language when applying for a job:

CV (curriculum vitae): a brief account of someone's career which gives details of their qualifications and experience

master's: a second degree usually shortened to MA (master of arts) or M.Sc. (master of science)

marketing: the job of selling or promoting a product

21 Do sit down ... (continued)

Listen again to the interview and complete the notes the interviewer makes.

Post: Marketing Director

Interviewee: Chris Clarkson

Qualifications: (1) _____ degree and M.A. in

(2) _____ from US

Experience: (3) _____ _____ with Proton Designs

Reasons for wanting job:

   1. Company is too (4) _____

   2. Wants more (5) _____ work.

Good points:

   1. Speaks (6) _____ and (7) _____

   2. Responsible for developing (8) _____

   _____

Test tip: In this test you are listening out for specific details. Read the gapped notes and decide what type of information you are listening for. In gap (1) you are listening for a type of degree. Think about the types of degree you know about.

22 John and Jessie

Listen to this interview with John and Jessie and decide if the statements belong to John or Jessie or neither of them.

	John	Jessie	Neither
I liked sport best.	✓		
I found schoolwork difficult.			
I used to mess about in lessons.			
I sometimes forgot to do my homework.			
I was bored at school.			
I liked chemistry lessons best.			
I was happy when I left school.			
I liked my English teacher.			
I think school is harder than going to work.			

Some common slang words:

skive off: avoid lessons

goody-goody: someone who appears well-behaved (in an irritating way)

cool: good fun

23 Supermodel

Listen to this radio interview between a psychiatrist and a supermodel and choose the best answer – a, b or c – for each question.

1 The psychiatrist says that many people who come on the programme

a) believe they have had wonderful childhoods.
b) found it easier to make money because of their looks.
c) wish they had been born beautiful.

2 What does the psychiatrist find hard to believe?

a) Agnetta's mother was beautiful.
b) Agnetta was not a beautiful child.
c) Agnetta was glad her mother was beautiful.

3 Why did Agnetta think it was fortunate that she was an ugly child?

a) She had to try harder to be loved.
b) It made her relationship with her father stronger.
c) It helped her cope with being beautiful later on.

4 Why does Agnetta believe her mother's departure was a good thing?

a) Her father was much happier.
b) She didn't feel so ugly any more.
c) It made her keener to succeed.

5 What does the psychiatrist think about Agnetta now?

a) Her experience has made her strong.
b) She still feels ugly and unloved.
c) She has not been greatly affected by her loss.

Some useful words for talking about lifestyles:
idyllic: extremely happy
supermodel: famous and successful model
acceptable: liked by other people
affected: influenced

24 Superhead

Listen to this interview with a headmaster of a school. Match the words 1–7 to those listed a–g to show you understand their meaning in the recording.

1	deprived	a	harmed
2	resign	b	disappoint
3	behaviour	c	disadvantaged
4	troublemaker	d	leave
5	damaged	e	environment
6	let down	f	nuisance
7	setting	g	conduct

superhead: In the UK a 'superhead' is a special teacher sent into a school which is having difficulties in order to improve the education the pupils are getting and to deal with problems such as bad behaviour.

school governors: Every state school in the UK has a board of governors whose job is to appoint teachers and make other important decisions about the school.

education authority: These are local administrative bodies in charge of school education in the UK.

25 Superhead (continued)

Listen to the interview again and decide if the statements are true or false.

1 Mr. Tørstig was invited to be the head teacher of a school. _T_

2 He thought he could improve the school. _____

3 He was backed up by the education authority. _____

4 Many children did not attend lessons regularly. _____

5 He was asked to leave by the school governors. _____

6 He wanted the most difficult children to go to another school. _____

7 There was not enough money to complete the building work. _____

8 The governors asked some of the teachers to resign. _____

9 Mr. Tørstig thinks the children did not want him to go. _____

10 He would have to think carefully before going back into teaching. _____

Test tip: The statements follow the order in which you will hear them. Read through them carefully before listening for the first time, decide if they are true or false and then listen again to check your answers.

26 Going for gold

Listen to this interview with a show jumper and choose the best answer – a, b or c – for each question.

1 The rider is disappointed because

a) he didn't win a medal.
b) he expected to win a gold medal.
c) he only got a bronze medal.

2 Why did the horse knock down the second fence?

a) The horse and his rider were not paying attention.
b) The horse lost a shoe.
c) The rider was blowing his nose.

3 What happened at the water jump?

a) The rider was feeling anxious.
b) The horse saw something in the crowd.
c) The rider fell into the water.

4 After the water jump he

a) made no more mistakes.
b) lost a further ten seconds.
c) decided to give up.

5 What are the rider's thoughts about the cross-country event?

a) He thinks he could win.
b) He prefers this type of event.
c) He knows it will be difficult.

6 How does the interviewer sound at the end?

a) Disappointed
b) Worried
c) Encouraging

 Test tip: In some of these multiple choice questions you have to complete a sentence. It is a good idea to read the stem sentence with each of the options before you listen to the recording as this will help you focus on the meaning of each completed sentence.

27 Going for gold (continued)

As you listen to the interview again find words and phrases which mean the following:

1 very upset

2 determined to get

3 failed

4 did not pay attention

5 fearful

6 catch up

7 abandoned the attempt

8 very difficult

28 Blackbirds

Listen carefully and fill in the gaps in this poem.

For some hours now
I've (1) _____ two blackbirds play
a tireless (2) _____ of tag
on the spare, black (3) _____ of an apple tree.
Saw and felt the tension.
(4) _____ the moment
till one gave way.

And (5) _____ in this dance,
repeated endlessly (6) _____ the stiff cold day,
has (7) _____ my thoughts together
letting the road between us
(8) _____ clean
swept of last year's sodden leaves,
and old griefs.

So as this day thins (9) _____
And the year turns,
I keep my (10) _____ and wait.

Test tip: The first time you listen to the verses and stories in this section don't look at the words. Decide what you think each one is about as you listen.

29 Blackbirds (continued)

A   Choose three phrases in the poem that tell you it is winter.

1 _____

2 _____

3 _____

B   Listen again and match words 1–7 to their meaning in the poem.

1	spare	darkens
2	sodden	thin
3	griefs	pull
4	tension	soaked
5	turns	ends
6	thins out	sadness
7	draw	tightness

30 The lottery ticket

Listen to this girl telling her friend about something that happened to her. Work out the correct order of the pictures, and write the letters below.

_d_ _ _ _ _ _ _ _

Test tip: Before you listen to the recording look carefully at the pictures and decide what is happening in each one. Think about how you would describe what is happening in a single sentence. Now you are ready to listen.

31 Ha, ha, ha

Listen to this joke and work out the correct order of the pictures. Then write the letters below. There are two pictures which are not part of the story.

— — — — —

 Here are some of the American words in this joke and their British
equivalents:

bunch: group

truck: lorry

guy: bloke (man)

bucks: dollars

takes off: leaves

movies: cinema (films)

32 The red coat

Listen to this story and complete the summary below with one or two words in each gap.

There was a man who was grieving for his dead wife. He went back to work as his (1) _____friends_____ thought this would help him. Every day he took the train to and from the city where he worked in a (2) _____. One day a (3) _____ got on the train and sat (4) _____ him. She started to do this every day but he only noticed her when she wore a (5) _____.

The man decided to go (6) _____. When he was out walking he noticed some red material caught in between (7) _____ at the bottom of a cliff. He climbed down but could not find the red material.

He went back to work and on his way home he (8) _____ the girl in the red coat but she did not get on the train. When he got home there was a (9) _____ for him. It was his wife's red coat which had been lost at the (10) _____. He cried for the first time since his (11) _____.

He took the coat to a (12) _____ and asked her if she would like it. He told her that he knew it was time to get over his loss.

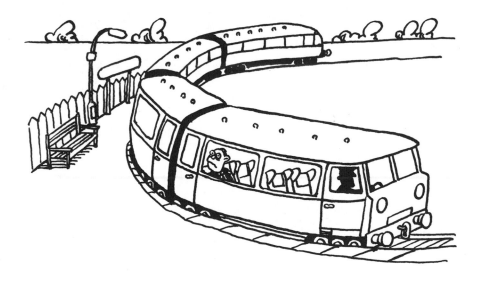

33 The red coat (continued)

Listen again to the story and answer questions 1–4 by choosing the best answer – a, b or c.

1 Why did the man not notice the girl on the train at first?

a) He was reading a newspaper.

b) She did not sit near him.

c) He was thinking hard about his wife.

2 When the girl did not get on the train

a) he missed her.

b) he was worried.

c) he forgot about her.

3 Why did he choose the island for his holiday?

a) It was famous for birds.

b) He hadn't been there with his wife.

c) He had visited it when he was young.

4 When he saw the piece of red material he was

a) happy.

b) excited.

c) anxious.

5 Why was the man looking forward to going back to work?

a) He wanted to see the girl again.

b) He had not enjoyed his holiday.

c) He wanted to talk about his wife.

6 What was important about the return of his wife's coat?

a) It was his wife's favourite.

b) It allowed him to grieve properly.

c) It reminded him of the girl on the train.

34 A dream

Listen to two people discussing a dream one of them has had. Decide which statements are true and which are false.

1	The woman has had a dream which she can't forget.	_T_
2	In the dream there are people trying to take a parcel from her.	_____
3	She drops the parcel when someone bumps into her.	_____
4	She decides to sit down and open the parcel.	_____
5	She is surprised to find the parcel contains a necklace.	_____
6	A man comes up to her and asks for the necklace.	_____
7	She does not want to give it to him.	_____
8	He runs off with the necklace.	_____
9	She feels a lot better when the necklace has gone.	_____
10	She asks her friend to explain what the dream could mean.	_____

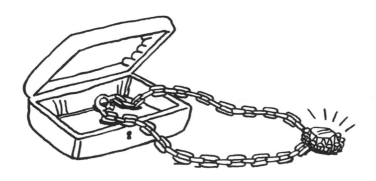

35 A dream (continued)

Listen again to what the dream could mean and answer the questions by choosing the best answer – a, b or c.

1 In the dream the woman's responsibilities are represented by

a) the city street.

b) the people.

c) the parcel.

2 When the parcel falls to the ground she is

a) letting go of her responsibilities.

b) showing how tired she is.

c) saying she does not care any more.

3 The man who takes the necklace shows her that

a) she cannot trust everyone.

b) she has lost something important.

c) there are people who can help her.

4 It is important that the parcel contains a necklace because it

a) belonged to the man.

b) looks like a chain.

c) is very valuable.

5 The woman finds the dream useful because she now understands that she can

a) give up looking after people.

b) share her responsibilities with others.

c) look out for people who might hurt her.

Test tip: What do you think the dream was about? If you can, discuss the dream's meaning with someone. If not, write down a few sentences which explain the dream.

36 Office move

A Listen out for the words and phrases a–e in this discussion. Tick off each word or phrase when you hear it.

a pluses and minuses

b be good for our image

c along the lines of

d purpose-built

e look into

B Match the words and phrases a–e with the highlighted parts of sentences 1–5.

1 I was thinking more **about** a corporate dining room than a canteen. _____

2 It will **improve the way people think of us** if we move to the Innovations Park. _____

3 The human resources department will **investigate** the possibility of setting up a crèche. _____

4 What are the **advantages and disadvantages** of moving to the new site? _____

5 The building has been **designed specifically** as a factory. _____

Some business terms:

workforce: an organisation's employees

innovations park: an area reserved for building new business developments

shift: period of time worked by a group of workers which starts as another group finishes

financial implications: costs involved

crèche: place where young children are looked after while their parents are working

37 Office move (continued)

Listen again to the discussion and choose the best answer – a, b or c – for each question.

1 The meeting is to discuss

  a) arrangements for the company's move to a new site.

  b) the advantages for the company of moving to a new site.

  c) how to stop the company from moving to a new site.

2 Sam believes that a purpose-built factory will

  a) increase efficiency.

  b) improve their image.

  c) attract more staff.

3 Hannah thinks that if the company moves to the new site

  a) parking will be more difficult.

  b) a bus service will be essential.

  c) staff will have difficulty in getting to work.

4 Tom agrees with Hannah that

  a) the best staff will want to stay anyway.

  b) a bus service would be too expensive

  c) a new building would be good for the company's image.

5 If the company moves to the new site Tom wants

  a) a crèche.

  b) a canteen.

  c) a dining room.

6 Most staff at the company

  a) have school age children.

  b) are female.

  c) would use the crèche facilities.

Test tip: Read through the questions and each option carefully and make sure you understand each complete sentence. For example: 1a) *The meeting is to discuss arrangements for the company's move to a new site.* Think about how it is different from the other two options in each question.

38 Nightclubbing

A   Listen to this discussion about building a nightclub in a residential area and match the words and phrases you hear in list 1 to phrases with similar meanings in list 2.

List 1	**List 2**
1 going over it again	crowds
2 hordes	out of control
3 just not on	repeating it
4 have his say	express his views
5 a bit out of hand	not acceptable

B   Now complete these sentences with the words and phrases from List 1.

1   It's _____ to expect people to put up with all this noise.

2   There were _____ of young people waiting to go in to the nightclub.

3   The meeting soon got _____ as everyone was talking at the same time.

4   There's no point in _____ as we've heard it all before.

5   It's only fair for our guest to _____.

Test tip: Before you listen to the discussion read the words and phrases in List 1 **aloud** several times. Now listen to the discussion and you should be able to hear the words more easily.

39 Nightclubbing (continued)

Listen again to the discussion and tick those things which are mentioned in support of or against the project.

For the project

safe environment for young people ☐

employment ☐

help prevent crime ☐

strict laws to control noise ☐

lack of entertainment facilities

Against the project

too much noise ☐

litter in the streets ☐

bad behaviour ☐

drugs ☐

frightening for old people ☐

40 Holiday complaints

A Listen to the staff of a holiday company discussing some complaints they have received. Listen carefully and decide which phrase you hear from each pair of alternatives given.

1 loyalty and commitment *or* loyalty and assistance

2 made their wives miserable *or* made their lives a misery

3 was not amused *or* was not confused

4 came down with *or* came round with

5 concentration made *or* compensation paid

B Match the phrases you heard to their meanings.

a did not find it funny

b upset them a great deal

c a sense of duty and dedication

d a refund given

e became ill with

41 Holiday complaints (continued)

Listen again to the discussion and decide which of statements 1–8 are true and which are false.

1 It's the first time there have been complaints about the Hotel Splendide. _F_

2 Mr and Mrs Silk were unhappy about the state of their room. _____

3 Mr and Mrs Norrish thought the family next door were very noisy. _____

4 The Silks and the Norrishes were not satisfied with the amount of compensation they received. _____

5 The Barnes family all suffered from food poisoning. _____

6 The company flew the family home early because the hospital could not treat them all. _____

7 The company has decided to end their contract with the hotel before the next holiday season. _____

8 Mr Algis wants to know how much compensation has been paid to customers. _____

Some vocabulary you will hear in this recording:
made their lives a misery: made them very unhappy
come down with: catch an infection
lost it: lost (his) temper or lost control (of himself)
a fracas: a noisy disturbance
read the riot act: told (him) off forcefully

42 Cookery competition

A   Listen to this TV programme in which three judges are discussing meals that three chefs have cooked. Match the words you will hear in List 1 to those closest in meaning in List 2.

List 1	List 2
concoction	overdone
drenched	splendid
glorious	mixture
overcooked	covering
topping	soaked

B   Now complete these sentences with words from List 1.

1   I'm afraid the meat has been _____ and tastes a bit dry.

2   This is a _____ way to serve a salmon. Quite delicious!

3   The vegetables were _____ in a creamy sauce.

4   It's an unusual _____ of vegetables and rice.

5   I particularly like the crispy _____ on this pudding.

Some common words used in cooking:

grilled: cooked under direct heat

baked: cooked gently in an oven

poached: cooked gently in liquid

roasted: cooked at a high temperature in an oven

43 Cookery competition (continued)

Listen again and complete the table by filling each gap with one or two words.

THE BLUE TABLE		
	Tessa's comments	Tim's comments
Grilled smoked salmon	not traditional	(1) __excellent__
Crispy cabbage & potato	(2) _____	delicious
Poached egg	just right	(3) _____
Butter & onion sauce	(4) _____	very good

THE YELLOW TABLE		
	Tessa's comments	Tim's comments
Baked Ricotta cheese	(5) _____	too sweet
Summer fruits	perfect	(6) _____
Raspberry sauce	(7) _____	a bit thin

THE RED TABLE		
	Tessa's comments	Tim's comments
Roasted vegetables	good combination	(8) _____
Ciabatta bread	(9) _____	a bit dry
Parmesan topping	(10) _____	not fresh

44 No more fleas

A   Listen to a vet giving instructions to a pet owner and match the words in list 1 with words of similar meaning in list 2.

List 1	List 2
peel	pat
tap	press
drip	strip
part	drop
squeeze	separate

B   Complete sentences 1–5 with words from list 1.

1   _____ the dog's fur so that you can see the skin.

2   The fluid will _____ back into the main body of the pipette.

3   _____ the fluid out on to the skin.

4   _____ back the foil on the pipette like this.

5   _____ the narrow part of the pipette.

45 No more fleas (continued)

Listen again and decide whether the statements are true or false according to what you hear.

1 One pipette will last three months. _F_

2 You must make sure there is no fluid left in the narrow part of the pipette. _____

3 To open the pipette you cut off the end with scissors. _____

4 You should put the fluid on the dog's fur. _____

5 You must not allow your dog to lick the fluid. _____

6 You need to rub the fluid into the skin with your fingers. _____

7 You must wash your hands when you've finished. _____

8 You need to repeat the procedure monthly. _____

Test tip: When doing true/false questions, be careful that your choice of answer is based on **what you hear**. Sometimes you may think you know the answer, but this may not be what the text says.

46 Making arrangements

Listen to a woman leaving telephone messages for five different people.
Decide who each message is for by selecting from the people listed in a–h.

a	the son of a friend	message 1 _____
b	her mother	message 2 _____
c	her doctor	message 3 _____
d	a store manager	message 4 _____
e	her boss	message 5 _____
f	her next-door neighbour	
g	her secretary	
h	a head teacher	

Here is some vocabulary used in this recording:

enough to last me: enough (of something) for a particular period of time

in touch: in communication with

in a bit of a state: very upset

on its way: in transit

47 Making arrangements (continued)

Now listen again and decide what each message is about, selecting from topics a–h.

a	receiving a delivery	message 1 _____
b	booking a holiday	message 2 _____
c	looking after a pet	message 3 _____
d	visiting a relative	message 4 _____
e	rearranging meetings	message 5 _____
f	cleaning the kitchen	
g	cancelling an appointment	
h	ordering some curtains	

48 Carmen's calls

You will hear four voicemail messages. Complete the notes with one or two words in each gap.

Carmen – some phone messages for you:

The (1) _____nurse_____ rang about your (2) _____. Can you give her a ring (3) _____ 3 p.m. today? Also she wants you to make an appointment with the (4) _____ for next week.

Alice rang about the (5) _____ on (6) _____. Apparently Michael and Jenny (7) _____ come so do you know anyone who would come (8) _____?

Kerridge's (9) _____ say your car is ready. Nothing too bad just the (10) _____ _____ and the rear (11) _____! P.S They're open until (12) _____.

Your husband's flight arrives at Heathrow at (13) _____. He's coming home (14) _____ _____. He thinks he'll be home by (15) _____.

That's all. Hope you had a good day.

Pat

Some useful phrases to do with phone calls:

take your call: answer the phone

after the tone: after you hear a sound

get back to you: return your phone call/phone you back

give someone a ring: phone someone

In British English the verbs *phone*, *ring* and *call* are all used. In American English *call* is the most common verb, though *phone* is used too.

49 Getting there

Listen to someone giving directions to a theatre. Put each number from the map next to the right place in the list.

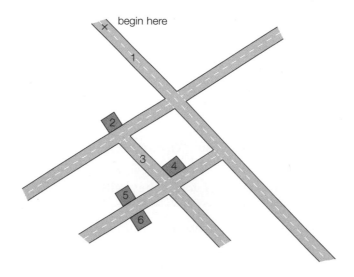

Royal Opera House   _____

Drury Lane   _**1**_

Bow Street   _____

cinema   _____

Floral Street   _____

church   _____

NCP car park   _____

Test tip: Listen to the recording and follow the directions on the map without writing down the numbers. Listen again and write down the numbers.

50 Shopping by phone

Listen to these phone instructions and answer questions 1–7 by indicating which button you should press.

Which button or buttons do you press if:

1 you have got through to the company and you have a push button phone?

---

2 you want to buy something?

---

3 you have forgotten your customer number?

---

4 you want to see the range of goods they sell?

---

5 you want to tell them your customer number is 178042?

---

6 you want to complain to someone?

---

7 you want to send something back to the company?

Test tip: Read through the questions before you listen to the recording. The instructions may be in a different order on the recording. Listen again to check your answers.

51 Make a note of it

Listen to the message and complete the notes by putting one or two words in each gap.

TELEPHONE MESSAGE

For: Bill Wade

From: (1) _____ Whitely

(2) _____ in January. He wants to move them to the

(3) _____.

He also suggested reducing the (4) _____ _____
to one hour and leaving half an hour for a (5) _____. Can
you let him know what you think about that a.s.a.p?

Good news! He thinks there are going to be (6) _____
_____ . Could you let him have any (7) _____
by 10 January or get it done yourself and just (8) _____
them.

That's all – his contact details are in the seminar file.

Jean.

52 First day

Listen to someone talking to a group of new college students and then complete each gap in the schedule with one or two words.

Auckland (1) _____ College		
Induction schedule for all students		
Time	Venue	Programme
10.30 a.m.	Main Hall	Mr James Crosbie, College (2)_____ Introductions
10.45 a.m.	Main Hall	Miss Judith Benton, College (3)_____ (4)_____ and domestic arrangements.
11 a.m.	(5)_____	Coffee
11.30 a.m. –12.30 p.m.	(6)_____	Dr Randal and colleagues College rules and (7)_____ _____
7.30 p.m.	(8)_____ _____	Formal dinner (no (9)_____ or (10)_____)

Test tip: Read the schedule before you listen to the recording and try and predict what sort of information you are looking for. For example, in gaps (2) and (3) you are looking for the position each person holds in the college. Look at the other gaps and predict what sort of information you are listening out for.

53 First day (continued)

Listen to the talk again and underline the words which are stressed.

1	<u>First</u> of all, may I say an especially warm welcome to students joining us this term.
2	I am looking forward to getting to know you all much better.
3	Now I'm just going to go through the plan for today.
4	After that we'll get together again in the library.
5	It is, as I said, a formal dinner, so no jeans or shorts, please.
6	Well, thank you all for being so attentive.

Test tip: You may find it helpful to look at the transcript for the recording on page 81. Underline the sentences you are listening out for.

54 Changes

Listen to Ang talking about her life since she left Vietnam and complete the summary by putting one or two words in each gap.

Ang and her family moved to (1) _____ when she was very young. She and her (2) _____ found it quite easy to settle in but it wasn't the same for the rest of her family. Shopping was difficult for Ang's mother because she didn't (3)_____ very well. Her father soon found work in a (4) _____ but it was very different from his job as a (5) _____ in Vietnam.

The family found other things hard to get used to. In particular, her mother missed her (6) _____ and the more social life she was familiar with. Ang still finds the (7) _____ hard to bear.

Even now Ang's mother dresses in traditional Vietnamese clothes and only (8) _____ Vietnamese food. This makes Ang feel embarrassed when she has her friends round.

55 Changes (continued)

Listen again to Ang talking about her experiences living in a foreign country and for each of the questions choose the best answer – a, b or c.

1 Why did Ang have to help her mother with the shopping?

a) There were no Vietnamese people living near her.

b) There were no Vietnamese working in the stores.

c) There wasn't always someone to go shopping with her.

2 Why did her father find working in a factory difficult?

a) He couldn't speak any English.

b) He didn't have many friends there.

c) He had had a much better job in Vietnam.

3 Why are Ang and her brother more fortunate than their sisters?

a) They did not need extra English lessons.

b) They look more American.

c) They speak with American accents.

4 What has Ang forgotten about life in Vietnam?

a) Living close to other people.

b) The warm weather.

c) Wearing traditional clothes.

5 Why does she find it difficult to invite friends to her home?

a) Her parents do not have much money.

b) Her parents have not adopted an American way of life.

c) Her parents only know how to cook Vietnamese food.

Test tip: When you listen to Ang talking for the first time, think about the five topics that the questions are about. You will hear the topics in the same order as they appear in the questions.

56 Dressing smarter

Listen to this presentation and decide if statements 1–8 are true or false according to the speaker.

1   The presenter wants to look informal.

2   He believes it's important to wear fashionable clothes.

3   He thinks there are times when wearing shorts is OK.

4   He accepts that a suit is necessary when meeting clients.

5   On 'dress-down Fridays' employees can wear anything they want.

6   People working in IT are the most informal dressers.

7   Many people who work in banks wear suits every day of the week.

8   Companies provide uniforms for their workers to make them more efficient.

Test tip: Make sure you understand what each statement means before you listen to the recording. Try and rephrase each statement in your own words.

57 Dressing smarter (continued)

Listen again and choose the right noun from the box to follow each modifier in the list.

1 general _____

2 interesting _____

3 specific _____

4 particular _____

5 dark _____

6 recent _____

7 fashion _____

8 formal _____

statement	presentation	trend	image	public
	occasions	day	suit	

58 A ghostly visitor

Listen to this man telling a group of people about a haunted house. Decide whether the statements about the ghost are true or false.

1	He comes into the room from the garden.	_T_
2	He plays Mozart on the piano.	_____
3	He doesn't frighten people.	_____
4	He is always smartly dressed.	_____
5	He sometimes says 'Good morning' to visitors.	_____
6	He walks straight through the mirror.	_____
7	He doesn't disturb anything.	_____
8	He was probably the gardener.	_____

59 A ghostly visitor (continued)

A   Listen again and match the words in list 1 to their meanings in list 2.

List 1	**List 2**
mistook	throw
put out	confused one thing with another
spooky	poorly dressed
chuck	offended
shabby	frightening

B   Now complete sentences 1–5 with words from List 1.

1   Don't _____ out anything that belongs to me.

2   She looked rather _____ in her old clothes.

3   He _____ a toadstool for a mushroom and was very ill.

4   She was most _____ by his rudeness.

5   It was a _____ old house so they didn't want to stay there.

60 Holidays

Listen to these five short monologues about holidays. From the eight sets of holiday makers below, choose the most suitable people for each holiday. There will be three sets of holiday makers left over.

1   A honeymoon couple looking for a tropical island.

2   A group of teenagers looking for a bit of a challenge.

3   Two friends who want to get out and about and do some gentle exercise.

4   An older couple interested in museums and architecture.

5   A young couple who want a week in the sun with plenty to do in the evenings.

6   A man and his dog who want a country holiday with plenty of walking.

7   A family of four looking for a quiet, rural holiday.

8   A family with young children who want sun, sand and sea.

- All these words and phrases are to do with holidays:

  open sheep country: sheep are kept in unfenced fields

  cordon bleu cooking: the highest standard of cooking

  snorkelling: swimming under water using a tube to breathe

  hang-gliding: flying while hanging from a frame

  scuba diving: underwater diving with breathing apparatus

  break: a short holiday

  half-board: holiday where breakfast and lunch or dinner is included in the price

- Make sure you know the meaning of these colloquialisms too:

  four-legged friend: a pet, in this case a dog

  put your feet up: have a rest

  no sweat, no hassle: without any effort or difficulty

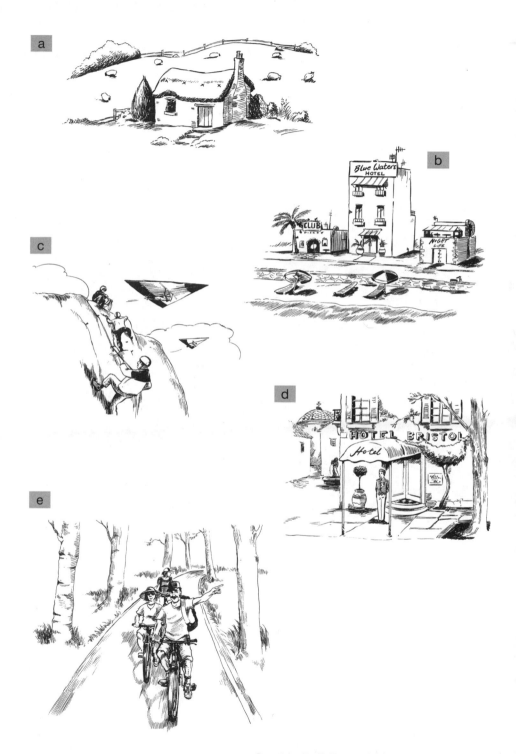

a

b

c

d

e

Transcripts

V1: = Voice 1

Section 1: Reports and announcements

Test 1

And now to round up on today's sporting fixtures. The soccer season is still two weeks away but there were a number of special matches which may give us some hints about future performance. Here are the results of friendly matches:

Lazio	2	Aston Villa	2
Leeds United	1	Athletic Bilbao	2
Newcastle	2	Everton	3
Ajax	2	West Ham	1
Ipswich Town	3	Blackburn Rovers	1
Arsenal	1	Chelsea	0
Manchester United	4	Manchester City	0
Real Madrid	2	Middlesborough	2

The match between Liverpool and Parma was postponed.

Tests 2 and 3

And now here's a round-up of what's on at the cinemas in your region this week. On general release from Saturday 15 May is the movie 'Gone in 60 seconds'. Nicholas Cage leads the gang as a retired car thief forced to do one more job. Highly recommended and has a 15 certificate.

Also on general release is a film for all the family, 'Toy Story 2'. This is an entertaining sequel to the original Toy Story. This time Woody is kidnapped by a toy collector. Showing from Friday 14 May with, of course, a 'U' certificate.

At selected cinemas only from 16 May with a 12 certificate is the latest Jackie Chan movie 'Shanghai Noon'. Set in the wild west this rather obvious story of murder and revenge is saved by its fighting skill and comic moments.

Finally I suggest you find the time to see 'Up at the Villa', a Philip Haas's adaptation of a novel by Somerset Maugham. Kristin Scott Thomas stars, with James Fox and Sean Penn as the men tangled up in her life. It's a 12 certificate and showing from 20 May at Chichester cinema and other selected cinemas.

Tests 4 and 5

V1: Suffolk police have issued a warning about two prisoners who escaped from Holsley Bay Prison near Woodbridge today. We are going over to our reporter on the scene, Oliver Johnson. Hello there Oliver.

V2: Good evening Jane. Yes, I'm standing outside the perimeter fence of Holsley Prison where earlier today two men, described as 'dangerous' by local police, escaped whilst returning from a work duty outside the prison. Fred Burke is forty-nine and currently in his sixth year of an eleven year sentence for armed robbery and manslaughter. During that robbery of a jeweller's one man was fatally injured. Burke is one metre eighty tall, of medium build with short, dark hair, brown eyes and a tattoo of a snake on his left forearm. The other prisoner is Ken Murray who is fifty-six, bald with a well-trimmed grey beard and a scar on his left cheek. He is only one metre seventy tall but weighs 100 kilos. Murray is serving twelve years for the brutal murder of his wife some five years ago. The police say that if you see either of them you should not approach them. Instead you should ring the following number: 01464 723955. This is Oliver Johnson returning you to the studio.

Tests 6 and 7

Announcement 1

This is a security announcement. A small black holdall has been left at the entrance to Gate eighteen. If you are the owner of this holdall please make yourself known immediately to our security officers.

Announcement 2

Will the owner of a light blue Ford Orion, vehicle registration number V 184 KDX, please go to the customer information desk at the front of the store.

Announcement 3

Could Mr Sadiki, recently arrived from Singapore, please go to the passengers' meeting point in the arrivals hall.

Announcement 4

We would like to apologise for the late departure of AA 479. If passengers present their boarding cards at the check-in desk, they will receive meal vouchers to the value of £5 per person.

Announcement 5

This is a staff announcement. Could Mr Baker please go to check-out number eleven.

Announcement 6

This is a customer announcement. We would like to remind customers that it is blue cross day. All goods marked with a blue cross are half-price today. Take advantage of this offer now.

Tests 8, 9 and 10

Reports are coming in of a lone yachtsman who has been picked up in the Atlantic Ocean. Hans Kühlemeier from Germany had been attempting to cross the Atlantic single-handed when he ran into heavy weather just off the Irish coast. He is said to be well but cold and hungry.

Fuel prices are in the news again as major oil companies are putting up their prices for the second time this year. This latest hike has drawn criticism from motoring organisations and road hauliers throughout Europe. The government is hoping to meet with oil executives later this month but this will be too late to prevent increases at the pumps.

After several days of heavy monsoon rain in India the government has now declared the east of the country a disaster zone. Aid agencies are concentrating their efforts on restoring fresh water supplies and distributing medicines.

Finally a story to ruffle your feathers. A lorry carrying 20,000 newly-hatched chickens shed its load whilst disembarking from a ferry at a small port in Thailand. Local workers from a basket weaving factory ran out and caught the chicks in their baskets. The driver was not happy when the workers tried to sell the chickens back to him. It gives a whole new meaning to 'chicken in a basket'!

And that's the headlines for Thursday 24 September. News in more detail is at six o'clock.

Test 11

Here is the world forecast summary for today, August 13. First for the eastern Pacific. Tropical storm Hector is gaining strength and looks like it may turn into a hurricane. It is presently located about 710 miles south-west of Cabo San Lucas in Mexico and is moving slowly westward toward Hawaii. At present it has winds of around 65 mph.

In the central Atlantic hurricane Alberto is moving into colder Atlantic waters and losing strength. This trend should continue for the next 48 hours. Alberto's maximum winds are now down to 90 miles per hour, gusting up to 110. That's still strong if it was near land but right now it's located about 980 miles west of the Azores and moving north-eastwards at 18 mph.

In the western Pacific tropical storm Ewiniar is only 230 miles south-east of Tokyo and it's moving northwards at about 15 mph. It's strengthened a bit, with gusts to 60 mph but it's also expected to begin to weaken as it heads out to sea.

In Australia a weak storm and its associated cold front is bringing scattered showers to Brisbane and Sydney and steadier rainfall to Melbourne and Adelaide. It will clear up by mid-week.

Finally for Europe, showers around Great Britain and in the northern Alps down to Florence and up into western Austria. Otherwise not a bad European summer; highs in the 80s in most of Europe and up into the 90s in Spain.

Section 2: Conversations and monologues

Test 12

V1: So what's the matter with you then?

V2: Oh, nothing. I'm just a bit fed up really.

V1: Why's that? I thought you were pleased about the new job and going to London.

V2: I am, I am. It's just that I've been here for so long in this town and it's hard to think of anywhere else as home. You know the worst thing will be not being able to take a walk with the dog whenever I feel like it.

V1: Yes, I can understand that. But I'm sure once you are settled in you'll be fine.

V2: Sure but you know it's not the same as being here. I've still got friends here, I know where the local shops and cinemas are and of course I've got you to look after me!

V1: Well, Tim, is that all you'll miss me for? Doing your washing and ironing ...?

V2: No, of course not, Mum. There's your cooking as well!

V1: Thanks a lot, Tim! Anyway when are you leaving?

V2: Tomorrow evening. I've got Simon to give me a lift with all my stuff. It's a pity he's not working in London.

V1: That's good of your brother. And the job?

V2: I start on Monday. I don't know whether to wear a suit or not. What do you think?

V1: Probably a good idea on your first day.

V2: Suppose so. I can't bear wearing suits.

V1: You look great in a suit.

V2: Oh, Mum, do you have to say things like that.

V1: Yes, I'm here to say the most embarrassing things to my teenage son. Anyway, it's only a summer job. You'll be back in a couple of months.

V2: True. Thanks Mum. Can I borrow your laptop? It would be so useful.
V1: Tim!
V2: Only joking, Mum!

Test 13
V1: Good morning Mr. Jenkins. What can I do for you?
V2: I've come about my foot. I think I've damaged it.
V1: Aha. How did you do that then?
V2: I think it was when I was playing my guitar. Sounds stupid, doesn't it?
V1: Well . . . What happened exactly?
V2: My dog came in and I tripped over her. Didn't see her and now I'm in agony.
V1: I'd best have a look then. Can you take your socks and shoes off, please?
V2: But it's only the right one that's affected.
V1: I need to compare them.
V2: I don't think there's much to see. Ouch!
V1: Tender there, is it?
V2: You bet!
V1: And does it hurt when I bend your toes?
V2: No.
V1: And what about your ankle?
V2: I don't think so.
V1: Good. Well this foot is definitely bigger than your other one. You may have broken a small bone but it could just be a bad sprain. You'll need an X-ray. In the meantime, don't put any weight on it.
V2: How can I get home then?
V1: We can lend you some crutches and you'll need a taxi to get you to the hospital. The receptionist will make an appointment for you but I'd like it to be as soon as possible.
V2: Thanks, doctor.

Tests 14, 15, 16 and 17
Recording 1
I suppose the worst thing about this job is the unsocial hours. The pay's good and the work is interesting but I can't stand the late shift. Of course, that's when a lot of criminals are active so it's a busy time as well.
Recording 2
I have to be very disciplined with myself. At nine in the morning I lock myself away with the computer and work until midday. Then I take a break for an hour and it's back to the office until five or so. I'm not usually lonely but I really miss talking to real people sometimes.
Recording 3
This place has been open for nearly sixty years. My great-grandfather set the business up. We were the only grocer's in town then. My grandfather and father worked here. I joined the army and spent twenty years seeing the world. Lived all over I have. Loved it! Never thought I'd end up here.
Recording 4
It's what I always dreamed of doing. I'm meeting well-known people every day and I'm being watched by millions of viewers. It's fantastic! I can't really believe it's happening.

Recording 5
There's no money in it these days. It's hard work and there's always something needs doing whatever the weather or time of year. We've got sheep and a small herd of dairy cattle and then my wife, she runs the bed and breakfast in the summer.

Recording 6
You've got to like people in this job and you've got to find time to talk to them. They don't just come in for a meal. They come to chat. We get a lot of people on holiday and they want to find out about the area and so on. I'm happy to oblige.

Test 18

V1: If I became a millionaire I'd first of all buy my mummy and daddy a big house and a swimming pool. And then I'd get a car for my brother. He's only four but he likes cars.
V2: Would it be a sports car?
V1: No, 'cos he can't drive yet. It would be a plastic one, not a real one. It has to fit in the garden as he's too young to drive on the road.
V2: Of course, I didn't think of that. And what about you?
V1: I will buy a big cage and keep hamsters in it.
V2: How many?
V1: At least ten. I like hamsters and cats and dogs. And then I'd buy some nuts for them. The hamsters, I mean.
V2: And would there be any money left after that?
V1: Yes, a bit.
V2: And would you save that for when you're older?
V1: No. I would spend it next week on, on …
V2: On another pet?
V1: No, I think ten hamsters is a lot so I'd pay for a taxi.
V2: A taxi?
V1: Yes and then my mummy doesn't have to take me to school in the rain any more.
V2: I see. You are a kind little girl.

Test 19

1 A I'm starting a new job on Monday.
   B Are you? How exciting.
2 A There's a new film on at the cinema. Do you want to go?
   B Yes, I'd like that. Do we need to book?
3 A The class is cancelled tonight. The teacher had an accident on the way.
   B Oh dear. Is she all right?
4 A There's a party at Tom's tonight.
   B Great. Am I invited?
5 A I'm getting married in the summer.
   B That's wonderful.
6 A My results should be out tomorrow.
   B Really? You must be worried.
7 A There's a new student arriving today.
   B Is there? I hope it's a girl.
8 A I think there's a car coming up the drive.
   B Right. I'll get my camera.

Section 3: Interviews

Tests 20 and 21
V1: Good morning, Mr Clarkson. Please sit down.
V2: Thanks.
V1: I wonder if you could start off by telling me a bit about yourself.
V2: Yes, er well, I took a science degree in chemistry actually but I didn't want to stay in that field so I took a master's in marketing.
V1: That was in the States, I see. And since then you've been working for a design company?
V2: That's right. I've been with Proton Designs for three years now. I think it's time to move on.
V1: Could you say a bit more about that?
V2: Well it's been a very interesting three years and I've learnt a lot. But it's a very small company and I'm looking for more of a challenge.
V1: And you think we can offer you that?
V2: I hope so. Certainly the job of international marketing director seems to be what I'm looking for. As you can see from my CV I can speak Spanish and French.
V1: Yes, that could be useful to us. Do you think you have enough experience for this post? After all, you have only three years marketing behind you.
V2: I know that doesn't seem much but I was playing a leading role with Proton. It is a small company so I was given a lot of responsibility.
V1: Such as?
V2: For example, I was in charge of developing a marketing plan for the company.
V1: That sounds impressive. Now perhaps I'll tell you a bit more about the sort of person we are looking for and you can see how you might fit in . . .

Test 22
V1: So, did you like going to school when you were young?
V2: I liked the sport but I wasn't any good at lessons. I used to skive off and go and play football in the park whenever I could get away with it.
V3: Did you? I was far too much of a goody-goody. I always went to lessons and did my homework on time. I didn't enjoy it though.
V1: So what was that all about? What made it such an unpleasant experience for you?
V2: For me it was having to sit still and concentrate. Actually, I couldn't concentrate. I was always getting into trouble for talking to my friends or scribbling on my text books. Once I took a pet mouse into a chemistry lesson and put it on a girl's lap and she dropped this test tube and it smashed. It was cool but it didn't go down well with the teacher.
V3: Yes, I remember that. It was Christine Boldy, wasn't it? I hated chemistry and maths. I wasn't any good at them and so I got bored. In fact most lessons were boring except English.
V1: Why was that?
V3: Don't know, really. The teacher we had when I was fifteen, she was nice. And I suppose I liked reading the books we had to study. I still like reading.
V2: I liked English because I could pretend to read while I was doing something else. I even went to sleep once and the teacher didn't notice!
V1: So you were glad to leave school then?

V3: No. I missed my friends, and the job I did when I left – I started working in a shop – was hard. I had to work weekends and evenings.

V2: That's the trouble. When you're at school you think it's boring and you don't want to be there but when you have to go and get a job you realise that it was OK really. I mean you could be with your friends and that and there wasn't that much hard work to do.

V3: That's right.

Test 23

V1: It's amazing how many people I interview for this programme tell me what idyllic childhoods they had and I wonder if my guest today will say the same. She's Agnetta Linstrom, supermodel. Agnetta, welcome to our studio. You are indeed a very beautiful woman. Clearly it's made you a lot of money. Are you glad you were born beautiful?

V2: Actually, I wasn't born beautiful. My mother was a very good-looking lady so everyone was surprised. I was such an ugly little thing.

V1: That's hard to believe. So your mother was very attractive and you were not and you remember this. Was this difficult for you?

V2: Not at all. Until I was five everything was perfect. In a way it was good not to be a pretty child. I had to try harder.

V1: Try harder?

V2: Yes. I had to work hard to make people love me.

V1: That sounds a strange thing for a child to have to do. What happened to end this happy childhood?

V2: My mother went away. I mean she left my father and me for someone else.

V1: That must have changed things.

V2: Yes. I was sad for a long time but it also helped me to be strong. I worked harder at being good at things. I still do and that's why I am where I am now.

V1: That's very interesting. It's as if you learnt when you were very young how to make yourself acceptable to others. And you still do that.

V2: I don't mind that. I am who I am.

V1: Do you mean, perhaps, you are still that ugly little girl who lost a beautiful mother?

V2: It could be. Yes, I think inside I am an ugly little girl.

V1: Perhaps too ugly to be loved by her mother.

V2: No, no but it is important to be loved.

V1: You sound sad when you say that.

V2: Yes.

V1: And now you are beautiful, rich and successful.

V2: Yes, I am. (hesitantly)

V1: You sound as if it's not quite enough.

V2: It is never enough, is it?

V1: No. So Agnetta let us look at your life now . . .

Tests 24 and 25

V1: So when you were asked to take on the role of 'Superhead', as it's come to be known, of this school which had 'failed' its children, you didn't hesitate?

V2: Of course, I thought about it but I love teaching and I like children and I thought I could make a difference.

V1: But these were some of the most difficult children you could meet, the school is in a very deprived area. Surely this was an impossible task?

V2: Nothing is impossible if you have the support of others and you can get the children on your side.

V1: But you did fail. You resigned after two years.

V2: I don't think I failed but I knew that I didn't have the full support of the education authority or the school governors. So I decided to resign. It was a difficult decision.

V1: But why do you think you didn't fail then?

V2: Because I think things were getting better. You could see it in the behaviour of the children. Before I started there was a serious problem with class attendance. By the time I left only a few children were still not attending on a regular basis.

V1: These were, I take it, the real troublemakers.

V2: I would prefer to say they were the most damaged children. They needed most help and I couldn't give it to them in that setting.

V1: What do you mean?

V2: They needed to be in a separate institution with smaller classes and more individual attention.

V1: And you weren't allowed to do this?

V2: No, I wasn't. I was told they had to stay in the school and this contributed to why the school did not improve as much as it should have done.

V1: And to your resignation?

V2: Yes. I was not supported in what I wanted to do.

V1: But other things were against you too. The school wasn't given enough money for new building work . . .

V2: Oh no, the money was there but the builders did not complete in time. We had to open the school while the building work was continuing. This was not a good beginning.

V1: And some of the teachers were not happy about what you were doing?

V2: Not exactly. However I did expect the teachers to support me and if they were not happy they could have left. When I suggested this I did not find that the governors agreed with me.

V1: So in the end you resigned.

V2: I did. But if I could I would go back tomorrow. I believe the children were sorry to see me go. I didn't finish my job. I let them down but there was no other way I could see.

Tests 26 and 27

V1: Well done, congratulations. How are you feeling?

V2: Devastated. I'm just devastated.

V1: But you did so well to get the silver.

V2: Well, I came out here aiming for gold. I got the bronze last time so I'm terribly disappointed.

V1: What happened? You were looking extremely good at the start.

V2: I blew it. The horse was going really well and then lost concentration. We both did.

V1: That's when the second fence came down. What happened at the water jump?

V2: My horse saw something in the crowd. It upset her. She can be quite nervous. That's what did it.

V1: At least you didn't come off.

V2: True but after that I couldn't make up the time. We lost nearly ten seconds getting out of the water.

V1: Considering that all happened so early on you did really well to clear all the fences after that. Some people might have given up at that point.

V2: I was determined to do it, to finish the round.

V1: So what now?

V2: Tomorrow it's the cross-country. That's going to be tough. Tougher than today.

V1: Well, I think you showed great determination today. Good luck for tomorrow and thanks for speaking to us.

Section 4: Poems and stories

Tests 28 and 29
Blackbirds

For some hours now
I've watched two blackbirds play
a tireless game of tag
on the spare, black branches of an apple tree.
Saw and felt the tension.
Caught the moment
till one gave way.

And something in this dance,
repeated endlessly along the stiff cold day,
has drawn my thoughts together
letting the road between us
appear clean
swept of last year's sodden leaves,
and old griefs.

So as this day thins out
And the year turns,
I keep my watch and wait.

Test 30
V1: You won't believe what happened to me yesterday!

V2: Go on. Tell me.

V1: I was on the bus going into town to do a bit of shopping and this man sat next to me. When the conductor asked him to pay for his ticket he looked in his wallet and there was no money in it. He was so embarrassed. I felt really sorry for him.

V2: Oh Judy! You didn't . . .

V1: Yes I just had to. I could see the conductor was annoyed. He started to tell the man to get off the bus. So I offered him the fare. It wasn't much.

V2: You're too soft. He probably did it on purpose.

V1: No, no I'm sure he didn't. But that's not the end of it. He got out at the next stop and when he'd got off I noticed he'd left a lottery ticket on the seat. I waved at him out of the window and showed him the ticket but he just smiled and went on walking. So I put the ticket in my pocket and didn't think anything more about it until last night. I heard the lottery numbers on the TV and just thought I'd check that lottery ticket. The numbers matched!

V2: Wow, Judy. How much have you won?

V1: I don't know but anyway it's not my ticket.

V2: Of course it is, he left it for you because you paid his fare. Come on Jude, let's have a look at it . . .

V1: I haven't got it.

V2: What do you mean? You haven't lost it?

V1: No. I felt awful about this man so I phoned up the shop where be bought it and they told me they think they know who it might be.

V2: So what have you done with it?

V1: It's under my pillow at home.

V2: Judy, you know something?

V1: What?

V2: You're mad. You could be a millionaire!

Test 31

This man had to take a bunch of penguins to the zoo for the new exhibit. On the way into town his truck broke down and he pulled over to the side of the road. A guy pulls up next to him and says, 'Hey, do you need some help?'

The man says 'Actually, all I need is to get these penguins to the zoo. If I give you fifty bucks will you make sure you take them?' So the guy takes the money and the penguins and takes off. The man went to fix his truck and an hour later he's pulling up into town to go check on the penguins. He stops at a red light and looks across the road and sees the guy walking with all the penguins following behind him. The man gets out of his truck and screams at the guy, 'Hey! What are you doing. I thought I gave you fifty bucks to get the penguins to the zoo!'

The guy turns with a big smile and says, 'I did take them to the zoo and I had some money left over so now I'm taking them to the movies.'

Tests 32 and 33

There was a middle-aged man who had recently lost his wife after a short illness. He was overcome with grief and his friends urged him to go back to work to help him forget. He worked for a bank in a city and every day he took the train from the small town where he lived into the city. It was a slow train and stopped at several small towns on the way. He always sat in the same seat next to the window and tried to read a newspaper.

One evening he was on his way home as usual. He was thinking about his wife and feeling rather sad. At the stop before his a young woman got on and took the seat opposite him. He hardly noticed her, he was so deep in thought. The next evening she was there again and this time he was aware of her because he caught sight of her bright red coat. It was a colour his wife often used to wear. The girl continued to join the train at the same station every day and usually sat in the same seat, if it was free, opposite him. He was a shy man and with the sadness he carried he did not look up when she sat down. However, on the rare occasions when she did not catch his train he hoped she would be there the next day. She usually was.

After about three months the man decided he needed a holiday. He didn't want to go anywhere that reminded him of his wife so he chose to go to a small island where he could walk and watch birds, something he hadn't done since he was a boy. It was a spring day with a sharp wind and rain in the air. He decided to walk to the other side of the island. It was not a difficult walk but at one point he had to walk very close to the cliff edge. The cliff path was narrow and dropped steeply down to the sea. He could see the waves breaking on the rocks below. As he stared down at the sea something caught his eye. It was a flash of red. He looked more carefully and then looked through his binoculars. The flash of red was in fact some red material that was caught between two rocks. His heart missed a beat and in his mind he saw the girl on the train trapped by her red coat. With great difficulty he climbed down the cliff face and towards the rocks. There was nothing there. He searched carefully for several minutes before returning to the cliff walk and his hotel. It was very strange but he felt quite upset that he had not found it.

The man was anxious to get back to work. On his first day back he could hardly wait until it was time to catch his train home. The girl did not get on the train. The next day he was even more excited although he was at the same time terrified that she might not be there. As the train drew into the little station he looked out of the window in both directions, hoping to see her red coat. There was no red coat. The train began its journey again and with a heavy heart the man sat back in his seat.

When he got home that night a neighbour called round with a parcel that had been delivered that day whilst he was out. He opened it and there in a neat bundle was a red wool coat – his wife's coat. The tears came and he buried his face in the warm, soft material. There was also a note from the dry cleaners explaining they had at last found the missing item and were returning it as requested. No charge would be made for the cleaning.

It was an important moment for the man. With care he folded the coat and wrapped it in paper. He took it round to a neighbour who knew his wife and asked her if she would like it. 'You see,' he said, 'it's time I let go. You've all been telling me that and now I think I can.'

Tests 34 and 35

V1: I had a dream last night which I can't seem to get out of my mind. I was walking along a city street carrying a heavy parcel. I wanted to put it down but I knew I couldn't. There were lots of people in the street who all seemed to be walking towards me and getting in my way. I had to get that parcel to somewhere important but these people were stopping me. I felt so tired and frustrated that I sat down on a seat and as I did so the parcel slid from my grasp on to the ground. As it fell the paper began to fall off. All that was in the parcel was a small box with a necklace in it. A man stopped and picked it up and said to me, 'This is mine, can I have it?' and I said yes and he went off with it. I felt a huge weight had been taken off my shoulders and when I woke up I still felt enormous relief. What do you make of it?

V2: Well, I think the important thing is the two feelings you describe. At first you felt weighed down by what you were carrying but when you were able to sit down and let go of it you saw that it was not so big and heavy and anyway you didn't really want it. You were happy to see it go. Am I right?

V1: I suppose so. And yes, I had no particular feelings about the necklace. It didn't seem to belong to me.

V2: So perhaps you have been carrying some feelings, some responsibilities around that you thought were necessary?

V1: Maybe. Yes, perhaps I take on too many things and usually I don't think about it too much and I get tired. I suppose the necklace is a bit like a chain.

V2: And maybe you did not realise that you did not have to be attached to this chain?

V1: Yes. And perhaps the man who took away the necklace means that I am not the only person who has to carry the responsibility or whatever it is. That seems to make sense.

Section 5: Formal discussions

Tests 36 and 37

V1: Hello Sam and Hannah. Do come in.

V2:)

V3:) Good afternoon, Tom.

V1: It's good of you both to come today. We really need to think about the benefits to the company if we move to the Innovations Park.

V2: It'll be great and I'm really looking forward to it.

V1: I'm afraid, Sam, that the final decision is out of our hands. Head Office wants to hear what we have to say but in the end . . .

V2: But it's such a marvellous opportunity. Just to have our own purpose-built factory would make such a difference to efficiency and . . .

V3: I agree that it would be good to have a brand new building but there is a down side you know. The Innovations Park is at least four miles from the centre of town. A lot of our workforce are going to be put off by that.

V2: I doubt that. If we were to offer a bus service at the beginning and end of every shift I think people would be keen to stay with us. If they're not that keen, well, do we really want them? Anyway there will be lots of car parking facilities and . . .

V3: We want their expertise and experience and their loyalty.

V1: I agree with Hannah that we have a good, solid workforce and we want to keep as many of them as possible. Your bus idea is a good one, Sam. There are financial implications but I'll raise that with the Chief Executive. Now any other pluses or minuses?

V3: I think it would be good for our image as a modern manufacturing company to be based in the Park.

V1: Yes, it certainly would and there'd be more space to entertain important customers. I was thinking along the lines of a corporate dining room rather than just a canteen.

V3: Yes, I'm sure that would be good for business. I'm still not convinced that people would be willing to travel out there for work. Many of them like being close to the shopping centre and schools and so on. That's important for our female staff and, as you know, 65 per cent of the staff are female.

V2: True, but there is a supermarket just up the road. Do we know how many staff have to pick kids up from school?

V1: Perhaps we should research that. I'll ask Human Resources to look into it.

V2: What do you think about a crèche, then?

V3: OK but it doesn't solve the problem for those who need to collect school kids. What about seeing how many are affected and then, if it is a problem, consider looking at the shift arrangements?

V1: Let's move on. Have either of you any thoughts on the accessibility of the new site for lorries and vans? How near the roads and rail services is it?

Tests 38 and 39

Vl: Welcome everybody and it's good to see so many of you have been able to make this meeting. Now we all know the topic for discussion so I won't waste your time going over it again. You will be pleased to know that Mr Claydon, who is the developer, is with us tonight. Perhaps I could ask you, Mr Claydon, to put forward your ideas about the project.

V2: Thank you. It is very kind of you to invite me here tonight to tell you about Blue Notes nightclub and disco bar.

V3: Look here Mr Claydon, let's get this quite clear: we don't want your nightclub or whatever it is. It's not because we're old and difficult. We just don't want the noise and the mess and we certainly don't want hordes of drunk teenagers on our streets.

V2: I assure you, nor do I, and that's why I think this club will be good for the neighbourhood. At the moment there's nowhere for young people to go. They get into trouble. This club will help keep them off the streets and stop some of that crime. It'll be a safe place for kids to enjoy themselves.

V4: Maybe it will but it's still going to be noisy. We're going to have our peaceful nights ruined by loud music.

V2: There are very strict laws to control the amount of noise we can make . . .

V3: And what's going to persuade us that you are going to be able to keep them, Mr Claydon? All we're in for is night after night of bad behaviour and fighting on the streets when you finally close. It's just not on . . .

V1: I wonder if we could just let Mr Claydon have his say and then we could ask some questions. It's all getting a bit out of hand at the moment.

Tests 40 and 41

V1: I'd like to begin by thanking you all for your loyalty and commitment to the company over the last few months. However we do need to look at the rise in the number of complaints we've been receiving. Jim, could you give us your report?

V2: Yes, er, we've had several quite serious, formal complaints from a number of people. In particular, there have been some problems with the Hotel Splendide.

V3: Oh no, not again!

V2: The most serious complaints were from two couples and a family who stayed there in July. Mr and Mrs Silk said that the room was dirty and the toilet was blocked. We moved them to another hotel after three days but it was further from the beach so they weren't too happy. Then a Mr and Mrs Norrish said that a group of young men in the room next door made their lives a misery with their noisy parties. In fact one of the young men apparently broke into their room one night and tried to get them to dance. Mr Norrish then lost it a bit and a bit of a fracas broke out. The hotel manager had to be called. He was not amused! Then there was the

Barnes family. They all came down with food poisoning after a meal in the hotel restaurant. The two youngest children had to go into hospital for a couple of days and then the rep had to get them an early flight home as they didn't want to stay any longer.

V1: Was any compensation paid?

V3: Yes. The Silks and the Norrishes received £200 and they accepted that. The Barnes were offered another holiday but we haven't heard back from them yet.

V1: Clearly we have problems with this hotel. I take it we won't be using them next year?

V3: That's right. Well, the rep read the riot act about food hygiene and told them the contract won't be renewed next year.

V1: Good. Well, Jim, I'd like a detailed report on all the cases where the company had to pay out money to customers. That includes costs of flights, holidays and so on. I shall need that information for head office by next Monday. Thank you everybody. That's all for now.

Tests 42 and 43

V1: Well, let's go over to the blue table where Stuart has prepared a wonderful concoction of grilled, smoked salmon on a bed of crispy cabbage and potato, topped with a poached egg and drenched in butter and onion sauce. Tessa, what do you think?

V2: This is not a traditional way of serving this fish . . .

V3: But it's excellent, mmmmm . . .

V1: Tim obviously likes it. What about the cabbage and potato? Tessa?

V2: Unusual . . .

V3: Oh it's delicious! And the poached egg is not overcooked.

V2: Just right – but the butter sauce is, well, just too fatty.

V3: No! It's very good.

V1: So, let's move to the yellow table where Donna has made a glorious pudding of baked ricotta cheese with a mixture of summer fruits and a raspberry coulis – that's a sauce to you and me – Tim, you're the pudding fan. What do you think?

V3: Well, it's a bit too sweet for my taste, don't you think, Tessa?

V2: I agree but the summer fruits are perfect.

V3 I think they are not quite sweet enough, actually.

V2: Oh Tim!

V1: And what about the raspberry coulis?

V2: It's a good colour and . . .

V3: A bit thin, though. I like my raspberry sauce a bit thicker than this.

V1: And finally to the red table where Chris has put together a delightful vegetarian meal of roasted vegetables on ciabatta bread (that's a speciality Italian bread that's getting so popular) with a Parmesan topping. Tessa?

V2: It is a good combination, isn't it?

V3: Unfortunately, it's a bit overcooked. Shame.

V1: Do you think so, Tim?

V2: But the ciabatta bread is an excellent choice and the topping, parmesan you said, is tasty. Mmmmm . . .

V3: I have to disagree with you, Tessa. I think the bread is a bit dry and I don't think the parmesan is fresh. It's come out of a packet, I'm sure.

V1: So, thank you both of you. We now have to decide who is the winner . . .

Section 6: Messages and instructions

Tests 44 and 45
It's a very simple procedure really. First of all remove the pipette from the packet by peeling back the foil like this. Take out one pipette, as you can see there are three in here so that's three months' supply. Then you have to make sure that the fluid is in the main body of the pipette. You do this by tapping the narrow part and any fluid that's got caught in there will drip back into the main body. See? Now you're almost ready to apply the stuff to your dog so make sure it's sitting ready for you. Now we have a very good, controlled animal here – aren't you, Beth? And what you have to do next is break back the top of the pipette, like so. Then part the dog's fur so that you can see the skin. Always choose somewhere the dog can't lick herself. This stuff is pretty toxic. So here between the shoulder blades is best. Actually it's not too good for humans, either. Make sure you give your hands a good scrub with soap and water afterwards. Now press the fluid out onto the skin. There's no need to massage it in at all. That's all there is to it. No more fleas. Make sure you do it every month, though.

Tests 46 and 47
Message 1
Hi Alex. Your mum said you wouldn't mind feeding Polly while I'm away. Could you use the back door and leave the key in the shed? She can go in the kitchen but don't let her into the rest of the house. She makes a terrible mess. Oh, and give her lots of strokes and she'll purr for you. Thanks a lot, I'm really grateful.
Message 2
This is a message from Renate Groves for Doctor Lewis. I'm sorry but I won't be able to make my appointment on Tuesday at four. I've got enough tablets to last me and I'll phone the nurse to make an appointment later.
Message 3
It's Mrs Groves here. I'm calling to let you know that Andrew is in a bit of a state about his grandmother who's very ill at the moment. I'm going to see her in South Africa next week and I'd like to take him too, if that's all right with you. I'll make sure he does some school work! Could you give me a call? Thanks.
Message 4
Karin, it's me, Renate. Just to confirm I'm away all next week. Could you explain things to the staff and postpone any meetings I've got? Thanks, I'll be in touch.
Message 5
Hello Mrs Hill. It's Renate from next door. I'm going away next week and I'm expecting a parcel. I've tried to cancel but the store says it's on its way. Could you possibly take it in for me? If there's a problem, let me know.

Test 48
V1: I am unable to take your call at the moment. Please leave your message after the tone and I will get back to you as soon as possible.
V2: Oh, hello. It's Nurse Peters speaking. I have a message for Carmen Sanchez. I'm expecting your results today and this is to remind you to give me a ring. It's probably best if you phone after 3 p.m. as we are less busy

then. The doctor would like to see you again some time next week so could you also make an appointment when you ring. Thank you, Mrs Sanchez.

V3: Hi there, Carmen. It's me, Alice. Could you get back to me as soon as you can? It's about the trip on Saturday. It looks as if Michael and Jenny can't come after all and I was wondering if you knew anyone else who'd like to come. I think it's too late to get our money back. Anyway, talk to you later.

V4: This is Kerridge's garage, John Barnes speaking. Just phoning to let you know your car is ready. No major problems just the brake pads and the rear lights needed replacing. We close at seven. Bye.

V5: Hello darling. Hope everything's OK with you. My flight is due in at Heathrow at ten this evening. Don't worry about picking me up. I'm going to get a taxi. Should be home by midnight. See you soon, bye!

Test 49

The Royal Opera House? Oh, that's not far from here. Go down this road – it's called Drury Lane – for about 100 metres. When you get to the traffic lights, turn right and take the first left opposite a church. That's Bow Street. There's a cinema, can't remember what it's called, about 50 metres along on your left. When you get to the cinema turn right into Floral Street. The Royal Opera House is a few metres further on, on your left. You can't park there but you can use the NCP car park on the opposite side of the road. You can't miss it. OK?

Test 50

Welcome to Shopping Direct. If you have a push button phone, please press the star key. Otherwise hold the line. Thank you.
If you have a customer number please enter the number now. Otherwise press the hash key. Thank you.
If you wish to place an order, press 1.
If you wish to order a catalogue, press 2.
If you wish to return an item, press 3.
If you wish to speak to customer service staff, press 4. Thank you.
All our staff are busy at present and your call has been placed in a queue. Thank you for waiting.

Test 51

V1: Is Bill Wade there please?
V2: No. He's out of the country until next week. Can I take a message?
V1: Yes, it's quite urgent. It's Roy Whitely speaking and it's about the workshops in January.
V2: Oh, yes. I know the ones you mean.
V1: Well, we're finding it difficult to find a venue for the 16th and I wonder if Bill would be happy if we made it on the 27th instead?
V2: He'll have to get back to you on that one.
V1: Also we were going for a morning slot and an afternoon slot of two hours each. I've thought about it again and I think it would be best to keep the afternoon to an hour, plus half an hour for a round-up. If he doesn't like the sound of that could he let me know?
V2: Yes, of course.
V1: It looks like we've got about twenty-two participants which is great. Bill

said something about duplicating handouts. Could he let me have anything he wants copying by the 10th? If he prefers he could do the duplicating himself and just invoice us. I think that's all.

V2: That's fine, Mr Whitely. I'll make sure he gets the message as soon as he gets back.

V1: Thanks. Bye.

V2: Goodbye.

Section 7: Talks and presentations

Tests 52 and 53

Good morning everybody. First of all may I say an especially warm welcome to students joining us this term. I am James Crosbie, the principal of Auckland International College, and I am looking forward to getting to know you all much better.

Now I am just going to go through the plan for today. You should have received your schedule already and, yes, I can see that most of you have it with you. Good. Now if you look at the arrangements for this morning you can see that when I have finished this introduction, the college administrator, Miss Judith Benton, would like to have a word with you about financial matters and other domestic details which will help to make your stay with us more comfortable. Then we will have a short break for coffee or whatever on the terrace. After that we will get together again in the library. I shall at this point hand over to my deputy, Dr Randall, for the rest of the morning. He and other colleagues will be telling you about the college and our rules (not that many, I assure you). Also there will be information about the social programme we have put together for the next few days. The rest of the afternoon is free for you to unpack and settle in but I would be pleased to see you all for the formal dinner tonight which will be at 7.30 p.m. in the dining hall. It is, as I said, a formal dinner so no jeans or shorts, please.

Well, thank you all for being so attentive. I hope this indicates how you approach your studies! May I introduce Miss Benton, our college administrator.

Test 54 and 55

I was a small child when I left Vietnam and moved with my family to live in America. For me and my little brother, it didn't take long before we felt American, but for my parents and two older sisters, it was a different story. The biggest problem for my mother was the language. We were living in New York and although there were quite a lot of Vietnamese families near us they didn't work in the stores. This meant my mother had to take me with her when she went shopping and I was usually at school.

For my father the most important thing when we arrived was to find a job. Luckily he had friends who knew us in Vietnam and they helped him get a job in a factory. It was hard for him to do that sort of work. In Saigon he had been a doctor.

My two older sisters went to high school. They worked hard and did well and the school gave them extra English lessons. Even now, though, they speak with Vietnamese accents. My brother and I are lucky. We may look Vietnamese but we speak with American accents!

My family found the way of life very different. In Vietnam my mother used to spend a lot of time visiting her sisters and brothers and looking after her mother and father. She feels quite lonely now. She says that in America you live inside your house but in Vietnam you take your house outside onto the street and share your life with everybody. I don't remember that but I do find the winters are quite hard to put up with in New York. It's very cold and snows a lot.

My mother still wears traditional Vietnamese clothes at home and always cooks us rice and noodles. I must admit I prefer burgers and chips! Although my friends like to visit us I often feel a bit embarrassed by my parents' way of life. They do not understand Americans and I think I am more American than Vietnamese now. I suppose it is sad for them to have such a strange daughter.

Tests 56 and 57

V1: Welcome everybody to this presentation about creating a corporate image for your company. I wonder if, when you came in today, you thought, 'Hey, this guy hasn't got a suit on. This could be an interesting day!' You see, I believe that the way you dress is very important. I decided to come here rather casually dressed not because I wanted to make a fashion statement but because I wanted to let you know that this is not going to be a formal presentation. On the other hand, I want you to work hard and get something out of the day. I'm not wearing shorts and a T-shirt, for instance. So how would you describe the way I'm dressed?

V2: Smart but casual.

V1: Exactly. But I also believe there are particular occasions when you need to wear a suit such as meeting a client – especially if you expect the client to be wearing one. Which brings me to a recent trend which we've picked up from the Americans: 'Dress down Friday'. How many of you are dressing more informally on a Friday? Quite a lot of you. How many of you go as far as wearing jeans? Not so many. Probably many of that small group work in the IT sector? I thought so.

So you see it's not just the day of the week or what clients may expect of you, it's the business you're in. If, for example, you work in a bank you're probably going to be in a dark suit every day of the week. And then there are those of us who are expected to wear a uniform. What you are doing here is projecting a very specific image of your company or service. Usually it's to do with reliability, expertise and efficiency. Customers and the general public feel reassured about someone in a recognisable uniform. Dress down Friday is a long way off for this group of employees.

Now let's have a look at other ways in which a company projects its image . . .

Tests 58 and 59

If you'd all like to step in here. Now this looks like a very ordinary sitting room, doesn't it? There's a piano so obviously somebody in the family plays. However, all is not how it seems. I am assured by Mrs. Martindale that quite often she has a ghostly visitor!

Apparently there is a gentleman who lets himself in through those French doors over there, sits himself down at the piano and plays a few tunes. Mozart, usually. Not at all frightening, I'm told. Quite a gentle looking fellow with long, grey hair and rather shabby clothes. One visitor mistook him for the gardener and was quite put out when he didn't reply to her 'Good morning'. Like all good ghosts he ignores everybody in the room, well, doesn't appear to see them. When he's finished his piece at the piano he gets up, walks over to the fireplace and looks into the mirror and straightens his tie. And now, this is the *spooky* bit: there is no reflection in the mirror!

Mrs Martindale, you'll meet her in a minute, tells me she quite likes having him around. He plays the piano quite well and doesn't interfere with anything. Doesn't chuck anything about or things like that. Her theory is that he used to live here and somehow didn't want to leave. Right, let's walk this way into the kitchen. I think we'll find some refreshments waiting for us.

Test 60
Holiday a
We offer self-catering cottages for a minimum of three nights. The cottages are open all the year round and children are welcome. Sorry, no four-legged friends are allowed as this is open sheep country.
Holiday b
If you are looking for some lively night life, and you're not too bothered about fancy bedrooms and cordon bleu cooking, this basic but clean hotel situated in the resort of Argassi on the island of Zante in Greece could be your choice.
Holiday c
Our activity courses are as varied and demanding as you will find anywhere. We have climbing and snorkelling weeks but for the more adventurous why not try hang gliding or scuba diving?
Holiday d
So you're not the beach type and prefer to spend time in more cultured surroundings? Then we have the perfect holiday for you. Our two city breaks, staying at five star hotels, are available on a bed and breakfast or half board basis.
Holiday e
Are you not very fit but would still like to do more than put your feet up on holiday? How about a holiday on two wheels? We provide the cycles and carry your luggage for you. No sweat, no hassle, we'll do all the planning and you can enjoy the freedom and the fresh air.

Answers

Section 1: Reports and announcements

Test 1
1 Arsenal
2 Manchester United
3 Ajax
4 Manchester City
5 Blackburn Rovers
6 Liverpool v. Parma
7 Chelsea, Manchester City
8 Middlesborough

Test 2
(a) 1 e   2 c   3 a   4 b   5 d
(b) 1 on general release
    2 round-up
    3 adaptation
    4 sequel
    5 selected cinemas

Test 3
1 in sixty seconds
2 15 May
3 car thief
4 general release
5 toy collector
6 Shanghai Noon
7 12
8 selected
9 murder
10 12
11 20 May
12 love story

Test 4
1 Fred
2 49
3 1m 80
4 medium
5 dark hair
6 brown
7 tattoo
8 snake
9 eleven
10 robbery

Test 5
1 Ken
2 56
3 1m 70
4 bald
5 grey beard
6 scar
7 twelve
8 murder
9 approach
10 01464 723955

Test 6
Airport: 1, 3, 4
Supermarket: 2, 5, 6

Test 7
checkout: picture 4
hold-all: picture 2
security officer: picture 1
check-in desk: picture 5
boarding card: picture 3
blue cross: picture 6

Test 8
1 c   2 a   3 b   4 b

Test 9
1 LONE YACHTSMAN PLUCKED
   FROM OCEAN
2 ANOTHER HIKE IN FUEL PRICES
3 MONSOON RAIN CAUSES FLOODS
   IN INDIA
4 CHICKEN RUN

Test 10
1 ran
2 concentrate
3 shed
4 disembarked
5 drawn
6 restored

Test 11
| 1 T | 2 F | 3 T | 4 F | 5 T |
| 6 T | 7 F | 8 F | 9 T | 10 F |

Section 2: Conversations and monologues

Test 12

1 ✓	2 ✓	3 ✓	4 ✓	5 ✗
6 ✓	7 ✓	8 ✗	9 ✗	10 ✗

Test 13

1 F	2 T	3 T	4 F
5 T	6 F	7 T	8 F

Test 14

1 c	2 e	3 b	4 h	5 f	6 d
7 g	8 a				

Test 15

1 c	2 f	3 d	4 g	5 b	6 e

Test 16

1 a	2 e	3 b	4 d	5 h	6 c

Test 17

(a) look after – care for
settle in – feel at home
trip over – fall over
take off – remove
end up – finish up
set up – arrange
set off – leave
pick up – collect

(b) 1 looked after
2 tripped over
3 end up
4 set off
5 pick up
6 set up
7 settling in
8 take off

Test 18

swimming pool
hamsters
cage
toy car
big house
taxi
nuts

Test 19

1 I	2 I	3 B	4 I
5 B	6 B	7 I	8 B

Section 3: Interviews

Test 20

1 start off
2 stay in
3 move on
4 looking for
5 working for

Test 21

1 science
2 marketing
3 three years
4 small
5 challenging
6 French/Spanish
7 Spanish/French
8 marketing plan

Test 22

	John	Jessie	Neither
I liked sport best.	✓		
I found schoolwork difficult.	✓		
I used to mess about in lessons.	✓		
I sometimes forgot to do my homework.			✓
I was bored at school.	✓	✓	
I liked chemistry lessons best.			✓
I was happy when I left school.			✓
I liked my English teacher.		✓	
I think school is harder than going to work.			✓

Test 23

1 a	2 b	3 a	4 c	5 b

Test 24
1 c 2 d 3 g 4 f 5 a
6 b 7 e

Test 25
1 T 2 T 3 F 4 T 5 F
6 T 7 F 8 F 9 T 10 F

Test 26
1 b 2 a 3 b 4 a 5 c 6 c

Test 27
1 devastated
2 aiming for
3 blew it
4 lost concentration
5 nervous
6 make up (the time)
7 given up
8 tough

Section 4: Poems and Stories

Test 28
1 watched   6 along
2 game   7 drawn
3 branches   8 appear
4 caught   9 out
5 something   10 watch

Test 29
(a) Any three of:
    spare, black branches
    stiff, cold day
    Last year's sodden leaves
    And the year turns
(b) 1 thin
    2 soaked
    3 sadness
    4 tightness
    5 ends
    6 darkens
    7 pull

Test 30
d, f, h, b, e, c, a, g

Test 31
c, f, e, b, d

Test 32
1 friends
2 bank

3 girl
4 opposite
5 red coat
6 on holiday
7 (some) rocks
8 looked for/searched for
9 parcel
10 dry-cleaners
11 wife's death/wife died
12 neighbour

Test 33
1 c 2 a 3 b 4 c 5 a 6 b

Test 34
1 T 2 F 3 F 4 F 5 T
6 T 7 F 8 F 9 T 10 T

Test 35
1 c 2 a 3 c 4 b 5 b

Section 5: Formal discussions

Test 36
(b) 1 c 2 b 3 e 4 a 5 d

Test 37
1 b 2 a 3 c 4 c 5 c 6 b

Test 38
(a) 1 repeating it
    2 crowds
    3 not acceptable
    4 express his views
    5 out of control
(b) 1 just not on
    2 hordes
    3 a bit out of hand
    4 going over it again
    5 have his say

Test 39
For:
safe environment for young people
help prevent crime
strict laws to control noise
lack of entertainment facilities
Against:
too much noise
litter in the streets
bad behaviour

Test 40
(a) 1 loyalty and commitment
2 made their lives a misery
3 was not amused
4 came down with
5 compensation paid

(b) 1 c   2 b   3 a   4 e   5 d

Test 41
1 F   2 T   3 F   4 F
5 T   6 F   7 T   8 T

Test 42
(a) concoction – mixture
drenched – soaked
glorious – splendid
overcooked – overdone
topping – covering

(b) 1 overcooked
2 glorious
3 drenched
4 concoction
5 topping

Test 43
1 excellent
2 unusual
3 not overcooked
4 too fatty
5 too sweet
6 sour
7 good colour
8 overcooked
9 excellent choice
10 tasty

Section 6: Messages and instructions

Test 44
(a) peel – strip
tap – pat
drip – drop
part – separate
squeeze – press

(b) 1 part
2 drip
3 squeeze
4 peel
5 tap

Test 45
1 F   2 T   3 F   4 F
5 T   6 F   7 T   8 T

Test 46
1 a   2 c   3 h   4 g   5 f

Test 47
1 c   2 g   3 d   4 e   5 a

Test 48
1 nurse
2 results
3 after
4 doctor
5 trip
6 Saturday
7 can't
8 instead
9 garage
10 brake pads
11 lights
12 seven/7
13 10 p.m.
14 by taxi
15 midnight

Test 49
Royal Opera House 6
Drury Lane 1
Floral Street 5
Bow Street 3
cinema 4
church 2
NCP car park 7

Test 50
1 */star   5 178042
2 1   6 4
3 #/hash   7 3
4 2

Test 51
1 Roy
2 workshops
3 27th
4 afternoon slot/session
5 round-up
6 twenty-two participants
7 duplicating/copying
8 invoice

Section 7: Talks and presentations

Test 52
1 International
2 Principal
3 Administrator
4 financial
5 terrace
6 library
7 social programme
8 dining hall
9 jeans
10 shorts

Test 53
1 First, all especially, joining, term
2 forward, know, much, better
3 just, plan, today
4 that, library
5 is, said, formal, jeans, shorts
6 Well thank, attentive

Test 54
1 America
2 brother
3 speak English
4 factory
5 doctor
6 family
7 cold weather/winters
8 cooks

Test 55
1 b   2 c   3 c   4 a   5 b

Test 56
1 T   2 F   3 F   4 T
5 F   6 T   7 T   8 F

Test 57
1 public
2 day
3 image
4 occasions
5 suit
6 trend
7 statement
8 presentation

Test 58
1 T   2 T   3 T   4 F
5 F   6 F   7 T   8 F

Test 59
(a) mistook – confused one thing
          with another
     put out – offended
     spooky – frightening
     chuck – throw
     shabby – poorly dressed

(b) 1 chuck
     2 shabby
     3 mistook
     4 put out
     5 spooky

Test 60
1 X
2 – holiday c
3 – holiday e
4 – holiday d
5 – holiday b
6 X
7 – holiday a
8 X

Test Your way to success in English
Test Your Vocabulary

0582 45166 3

0582 45167 1

0582 45168 X

0582 45169 8

0582 45170 1